# Of Mice and Men:

*A Reader's Guide to the John Steinbeck Novel*

ROBERT CRAYOLA

# CONTENTS

# INTRODUCTION

Welcome to *Of Mice and Men: A Reader's Guide to the John Steinbeck Novel.* In this guide I'll help you wrap your head around the book, and by the time we're done here you'll have a thorough understanding of it. We'll be looking at the story in terms of where it came from – the author and time period. We'll also look at the elements of literature that make up the story, examining each element individually to see how it plays a part in the book as a whole. And then I'll give you summaries of every section of the book, which you can use to clarify any confusing points, to help you remember the story, or to prepare yourself for reading the book if you haven't yet done so.

I will mention though, that if you haven't read the book, I will be going over every major plot detail. So if you don't want spoilers, go and read the book first! It's a very short book. If you don't care about spoilers, then read on.

**AUTHOR:** Let's begin by looking at the author, John Steinbeck. Who was he, and how does that relate to the book? We're only going to take a very general look at his biography, but it will show you that the story in *Of Mice* *and Men* really springs from his own experiences.

Steinbeck was born John Ernst Steinbeck, Jr., on February 27, 1902, in Salinas, California, right near where *Of Mice and Men* takes place. His father was a county treasurer, and his mother had been a teacher. Steinbeck was really encouraged in his reading and writing while growing up. The area where he grew up, Salinas, was very rural town with lots of farm land around. This exposed him to a lot of the farming community since he himself worked on farms in the summer for extra money. He got to see the way of life of these workers, their transitory existence, and that shows up in a lot of his works.

After high school Steinbeck began college at Stanford University in nearby Palo Alto. And although he attended for five years, until 1925, he left with no degree. From there he went to New York and tried to make it as a writer, but met with little success. He went back to California and worked in Tahoe City as a tour guide, and it was there he met Carol Henning, who he married in 1930. They moved near Monterey, California, and Steinbeck focused on his writing once again, and began to meet with some success.

In the early 1940s Steinbeck's marriage began to fall apart. He soon divorced and remarried a another woman named Gwyndolyn Conger. They had two children together.

Also, during World War II Steinbeck went overseas to work as a war correspondent in Europe and North Africa, but after being wounded in 1944, he returned home.

Steinbeck showed sympathy for liberal organizations throughout life, and was associated at various times with communist causes. He traveled to the Soviet Union in

1947, and as with many of his travels, he turned the trip into a book.

1948 was a bad year for Steinbeck. By that time his books had become more popular, but in that year he lost one of his best friends, the marine biologist Ed Ricketts, in an accident, and then was divorced by his wife, leading to a deep depression.

In 1949 he met Elaine Scott at a restaurant in Carmel, California, and they would be married a year later, and be together till his death.

Steinbeck continued to write a wide variety of material, and to travel regularly until his death on December 20, 1968. He had been a smoker all his life and had heart disease.

He was the author of 27 books and received the Nobel Prize for Literature in 1962. He wrote novels, short stories, nonfiction, and in a variety of genres.

**CONTEXT:** Context is where a book comes from. Now that we know a little about Steinbeck's life, we can look at the placement of *Of Mice and Men* in that life. It was published in 1937 and by then he had met with some success with books like *Tortilla Flat* and *In Dubious Battle*. If you aren't too familiar with American history, you should also be aware that the 1930s was the time of the Great Depression, when many people were impoverished and struggled just to feed themselves. Jobs were hard to come by and paid little, and we'll see that in *Of Mice and Men*.

The location is near Salinas and Soledad in California, near the Central Coast. It's a dry and hot region with many farms to this day. Steinbeck wrote this book while staying in Monte Seleno, California.

**STRUCTURE – THE NOVELLA**: Let's begin taking a look at the book itself. First we're going to look at the overall form. As I'm sure you've noticed, it's a pretty thin book, coming in at around a hundred pages, depending on which edition you use. A story of this length is considered a bit long to be called a short story, and a bit short to be a novel, so it's often known as a *novella*.

Also, Steinbeck wrote the book in the form of a "novel-play," so that it could easily be adapted to stage or film. There is a strong focus on dialogue and actions that can easily be shown visually, making it easy to adapt. And it was quickly and successfully adapted for both theater and film, and later television.

The book is divided into six untitled sections, and Steinbeck wrote the book with the thought of a three-act play in mind, with two chapters in each section.

**TITLE:** The original title of the book was "Something That Happened," but Steinbeck changed the title to a phrase from a poem by Robert Burns called "To a Mouse." The poem says:

*The best-laid schemes o' mice an' men*
*Gang aft agley,*
*An' lea'e us nought but grief an' pain,*
*For promis'd joy!*

And the language may be a bit odd to the modern ear because of Burns's thick Scottish dialect, and rendered in modern English reads like:

*The best laid schemes of mice and men*
*Go often awry,*
*And leave us nothing but grief and pain,*
*For promised joy!*

This is going to relate to the story, because several characters have schemes and plans that don't go as intended.

# CHARACTERS

**LENNIE SMALL:** Lennie is big and strong but unintelligent, possibly mentally retarded. He likes animals, mice, rabbits, and dogs. George is his only real friend.

**GEORGE MILTON:** George is small and has a temper. He is gruff, but he's smart. He bosses Lennie around and looks after him.

**AUNT CLARA:** Lennie's aunt, now dead. George knew her too, and when she dies, Lennie tags along with George.

**THE BOSS:** The ranch boss. Seems like a fair enough guy, but "has a temper."

**CURLEY:** The Boss's son. A short lightweight boxer with an attitude. He hates big guys and immediately takes a disliking to Lennie, and then George. Curley was recently married.

**CURLEY'S WIFE:** A woman who flirts with the ranch hands, very pretty. Curley seems very possessive of her and fears she will be unfaithful to him.

**SLIM:** The authority that the ranch hands actually work with (as opposed to The Boss). Described as friendly and fair.

**CARLSON:** Carlson is a ranch hand, a big guy, and he seems friendly. He takes on the task of killing Candy's dog.

**CANDY:** Candy is an old man, a "swamper." He cleans the bunk house and we also learn he can contribute $350 toward the land George and Lennie want to buy. He lets his dog be shot to death by Carlson.

**CROOKS:** The "stable buck." A black man with a crooked spine (the name *Crooks* comes from his crooked back) who works in the stables. He has some books, is good at horseshoes, and is intelligent. He is isolated in the barn, away from the other men in the bunk house, but also isolated in being the only black man there.

**WHIT:** A ranch laborer. He shows the others the pulp magazine with the letter from a previous laborer.

**AL WILTS:** Deputy sheriff in Soledad. Curley requests he come to the ranch after his wife is murdered.

**SUSY:** Runs the "better" whorehouse in town.

**CLARA:** Runs the competing whorehouse, described as "not as good."

# THE ELEMENTS
# OF LITERATURE

**PLOT:** Before I go any further into the elements that make up the book, let me give you a generalized idea of this book's story.

The story follows two main characters, George and Lennie, who work on ranches doing manual labor. Lennie has low intelligence and a child-like mind, but he's very large and strong. George is a smaller guy, intelligent, and acts almost as a parent figure to Lennie.

The book begins with them recently having left a ranch in Northern California. They had to leave quickly because Lennie had grabbed a woman's dress and frightened her. They arrive at a new job near Soledad, and quickly encounter conflict with the boss's son Curley, who is looking for a fight. Furthermore, Curley's wife flirts and talks with the men and infuriates Curley.

Over the course of a weekend, Lennie gets in a fight with Curley and crushes his hand. Later, while alone with Curley's wife, Lennie shakes her to keep her from getting him into trouble, and ends up breaking her neck with his great strength. He runs away.

The other characters pursue Lennie. George, being the one most responsible for Lennie, uses a gun to kill Lennie.

This was a very simplified outline of the story, leaving many characters and incidents out, but getting to the gist of the what the story is about. With this in mind, we can now delve deeper into the details of the book.

**NARRATOR & P.O.V.:** The narrator is the person telling the story. Who are they and what is their point of view? In *Of Mice and Men* the story is not told by an actual character, but by an all-knowing outsider who sees everything that takes place. We call this point of view "third-person, omniscient." *Third-person* simply means that it's not told in the voice of "I" because there is no character telling the story. *Omniscient* means all-knowing, because the narrator can see and know everything that occurs in the story.

**TENSE:** The book is written in the past tense, the standard tense for most fiction.

**SETTING:** The setting is the time and place that a story occurs. The time is the 1930s, the Great Depression. The place is at and around a ranch near Soledad, California. The story takes place over a few days.

**PROTAGONIST:** The protagonist or protagonists are the person or people that the story revolves around. Usually we can most sympathize or relate to them, and we care what happens to them. In this book the characters of Lennie and George are the protagonists.

**ANTAGONIST:** The antagonist is the person or force in conflict with the protagonists. We can simply name Curley as the antagonist since he harasses both George and Lennie. But we should also think about the nature of the economy and society that acts upon Lennie and George in a cruel way, and drives people to behave so viciously – this can also be viewed as part of the antagonizing force.

**CONFLICT:** There are several key conflicts to consider. Curley comes into physical conflict with Lennie and verbal conflict with George. There is also conflict between George and Lennie and Curley's wife, as they fight to stay out of trouble with her. And perhaps the deepest conflict is between George, himself, and society, as he struggles to handle Lennie, and ultimately forces himself to kill Lennie.

**CLIMAX:** Some people view the scene where Lennie breaks the neck of Curley's wife as the climax... but I disagree. The climax is the height of the story's tension, the point when the conflict is at its highest. After the climax, the story contains a falling action. But we can see that the death of Curley's wife doesn't end anything, and that the conflict is actually intensified. The tension is heightened as we wonder what will happen to Lennie and George. I think a better choice for the climax of the story is when George aims his gun at Lennie. This is the tensest point in the story, and once this has passed with Lennie's death, the conflict rapidly dissolves.

**RESOLUTION:** The resolution is how the story and conflict concludes. Sometimes it can resolve neatly, sometimes it can be sloppy and ugly. In *Of Mice and Men* the resolution is rapid. Curley is no longer the antagonist that he was. George no longer has to contend with Lennie. Slim escorts George up the highway to get a drink, and we're left feeling astonished, but relieved that at last it's all over, and nothing worse can happen to Lennie.

**TONE:** Tone is the attitude of the narrator toward the story, the "voice." For the most part, the tone is simple. Sometimes it verges towards the melodramatic or seem to moralize.

**THEMES:** Themes are the issues that the author is showing through the story. There isn't always an easy answer with themes, but they are what the author is contending with.

One thing we see a lot of – that comes through the title – is the idea of plans, ambition, and dreams. We learn of the dreams of several characters – George and Lennie, Candy, Curley's wife, Crooks – and all of those dreams are destroyed or fail to materialize. This is a pessimistic vision, reflecting the frailty of our dreams and the danger of pride and surety about anything in this world.

There is also a good deal about the cruelty people can do to each other, and the cruelty allowed by differences in wealth, position, and race. Curley, Curley's wife, and the whites (in relation to Crooks) all take advantage of their position to do wrong to others.

One more key theme is the relationships of friends or families. What is our responsibility to our loved ones? And what should we do when that responsibility comes in conflict with the demands of society? As we look at how people trust each other, we find no easy answers in this book.

# CHAPTER SUMMARIES & COMMENTARY

**SECTION 1:** The first section introduces us to a dry, hot central California near Soledad, along the Salinas river. It's very dry with small desert-like animals about... rabbits, coyotes.

We're introduced to Lennie and George. We get some exposition explaining why they're here (to get a job as manual laborers on a ranch). We learn of their relationship. George is the boss, and always seems angry about something, usually Lennie.

We get some recent history. They're coming from a ranch further north in California. They had to leave their ranch jobs there abruptly because Lennie fingered a woman's dress. He says he only wanted to feel the texture of the dress, comparing it to the fur of a mouse. Other men on the ranch probably thought Lennie was harassing the woman, but George got them out of there before they could be caught.

They also just got off a bus. George is angry because the driver could have driven them closer to their destination, but told them to get off too early and they had to walk four miles in the heat.

Lennie drinks the water in the river without considering if it's good water. We get hints that he has the mind of child, however much he looks like a man.

Lennie can't remember where they're going and why – this gives Steinbeck an opportunity for *exposition* – to tell us readers what is going on, since *we* don't know what their purpose or goal is. George reminds Lennie how they found the information for the ranch job and got bus tickets. Their previous job was near Weed, California, far up in northern California near the Oregon border.

They start to settle down for the night near the river. George discovers Lennie is carrying a dead mouse in his pocket. George throws it away. But when Lennie gets some twigs so they can start a fire and cook George's can of beans, Lennie picks up the dead mouse again.

We get to see that Lennie is a very simple soul, but George is the boss of the operation and Lennie does what he tells him. George hammers into him over and over that when they meet their new boss on the ranch, Lennie is not to say anything. George doesn't want the boss knowing that Lennie is unintelligent. He wants Lennie to work first and show the boss he's a good worker.

As we read and George says repeatedly how he'd be so much better off without Lennie, we have to wonder: Why then does he stick with him? And the answer is slowly revealed – George *does* genuinely care for Lennie. Lennie can feel George's anger and offers to leave him and go live in a cave, alone. But George knows that Lennie would never survive, with his limited intelligence. Lennie had also been complaining about a lack of ketchup for his beans, but to appease George he stops complaining and says that if he had ketchup he'd give it to George.

They talk about how they're so much better off than most ranch hands, who don't have anyone in their life, but they have each other. And they also discuss a fantasy they have of one day scraping enough money together to buy their own place and have rabbits for Lennie to take care of.

Their relationship reminds me of a lot of character duos like Laurel and Hardy, but more exaggerated, harsher, more realistic, stuck in reality, where stupidity isn't as funny, and men kill if certain mistakes are made.

We get hints (*foreshadowing*) that Lennie may be more trouble again in the future when George says, "You get in trouble. You do bad things and I got to get you out... You crazy son-of-a-bitch. You keep me in hot water all the time."

George recognizes that Lennie is ultimately a child and he has a responsibility to him like a parent.

Whether George actually believes their dream about living off the "fat of the land" with Lennie is up for debate. Perhaps it is akin to the concept of heaven, or salvation. George certainly uses this dream to help keep Lennie in check.

The chapter ends with the two men falling asleep near the fire and coyotes and dogs howling in the distance.

**SECTION 2:** The next morning has come and Lennie and George arrive at the ranch where they'll be working. They're led into the bunk house, where the ranch hands sleep, by an old man. It's a very drab, basic place. Each bed has an apple box near it as a shelf. Some of the beds don't have blankets, but instead have burlap bags. We get a glimpse of the life of a ranch worker. Steinbeck adds details of cowboy magazines and playing cards to give it an almost prison-like feel of monotony.

We get to see a lot of how George interacts with others in this chapter. He is not submissive at all. Anyone who gives him attitude gets it back in turn. Anyone suspicious of him gets his resentment. For instance, George is suspicious that his bunk has fleas and he's not afraid to show his suspicion and sneer. He refuses to be double-crossed, and as the situation that he and Lennie are in gets more tangled, he tries more and more to avoid getting cornered.

The old man who led them to the bunk house tells them about the boss. He say he's fair, but has a temper, and that he's angry they didn't arrive the night before. This description of a character before he or she arrives is a common technique in literature. It raises our suspicions and makes us keep an eye out when the character actually does arrive. We want to know if they match the description they've been given. "He's a pretty nice fella," they're told.

When the boss does arrive, he wants to know why they only arrived this morning. George exaggerates the amount that they had to walk from the bus dropoff. Last night he'd said it was about four miles. Now he says it's ten miles to make their tardiness seem even more unavoidable.

The boss is suspicious of Lennie's silence and eventually gets him to talk a little, to George's consternation. The boss senses something is wrong with the situation, and George tells some more lies. He says Lennie was kicked in the head by a horse as a boy, and that he's Lennie's cousin, justifying why he sticks by him.

George is slightly more respectful to the boss than he's been to other characters, but he refuses to ever be a pushover to anybody. Moreover, we see that he is a quick talker when he needs to lie, and he has no qualms about telling lies to save him and Lennie.

More characters are introduced, including Curley, the boss's son. And immediately we see that with his attitude there's a strong potential for conflict. The old man tells George that Curley is a boxer who likes to pick fights with bigger guys – and in this case, that means Lennie. A major conflict is foreshadowed, and we observe intently every action Curley does.

George and Lennie play cards until dinner, and George gives Lennie clear instructions regarding Curley. He is to avoid Curley at all costs, but if Curley attacks him Lennie is to fight back. Because of the inevitability of trouble, George reminds Lennie of the escape plan if anything happens: Lennie is to go back to the bushes near where they camped the night before.

We also get to meet Curley's wife firsthand. She is very pretty and wanders into the bunk house. Lennie is immediately fascinated by her beauty, but George sees her as nothing but trouble for them.

One theme we see a lot of already is the boundary between the rich and the workers. Those with money have more rights. Poverty is equated with far fewer rights, and the necessity of staying in an unpleasant situation simply to survive. The rich are also strongly equated with evil.

We also meet Carlson, a ranch worker, and Slim, the supervisor of the ranch hands. Even though Slim is an authority, he is far closer to the workers than the boss, and George and Lennie can relate to him.

Near the end of the chapter there is talk between Slim and Carlson about a litter of puppies that were recently born. When they leave, Lennie instantly lights up and tells George that he wants one of the puppies. Lennie's speech is always restrained around others because of George's orders, but Lennie is ready to talk when he's alone with George.

**SECTION 3:** We jump ahead a few hours and Lennie and George have gone to work in the fields. Lennie has fully demonstrated his value and power to Slim, who is impressed. Also, Slim has given Lennie one of the puppies from the litter

George and Slim get to talking, and George seems to respect Slim and starts to open up with what sounds like the real story about why George and Lennie string along together. George says both he and Lennie are from Auburn (presumably Auburn, California), and George knew Lennie's aunt Clara. When she died, Lennie just followed along with George and they got to working together. Lennie and George are the closest thing to family either seems to have. Lennie sees George almost like a father, and even though he is much stronger, he always does what George tells him. But having Lennie under him also gives George a responsibility for this powerful, but not so bright, person.

We also get more details about how Lennie and George left the town of Weed. Lennie apparently felt that woman's dress, and held onto it and wouldn't let go, ripping it off. It was reported he had raped her, when he had done nothing of the sort.

As Slim listens to all this, we get to see that he holds back any judgment and tries to get the full story. He seems to be a generally wise and friendly person.

Lennie comes in after playing with his new puppy, and George quickly sees that he has the dog concealed in his clothes. In this we see that Lennie really wants to follow George's instructions, but that he also has urges that he obeys and that he is capable of lying. George sends Lennie outside to return the dog to its litter, since it can't be in the bunk house.

We meet the old man again and learn his name is Candy. He has an old dog that stinks, and some of the others want to shoot the dog because it's getting old. Carlson says he'll kill the dog and it won't suffer at all. Candy is hesitant. The way they discuss putting a dog out of its misery will mirror later events when George must kill Lennie.

Whit, another laborer at the ranch, shows the others a pulp magazine with a letter printed from a previous laborer at the ranch. He'd written a generic letter and they're all impressed. At some point the dog is brought up again and Candy agrees to let Carlson kill the dog. Carlson leaves with the animal. When the dog is out of the building, the others try to play cards, but everybody is tense. They are expecting the gunshot sound that will tell them the dog is dead, and nobody can really act until they hear that sound. The shot is finally heard, and tension is released.

Slim leaves with Crooks to look at a mule's foot. Whit and George continue to talk, and the subject comes to Curley's wife, the way she eyes the workers and seems destined to have an affair. They also discuss Curley's ceaseless jealousy.

Talk turns to the prospect of visiting the whorehouse in town. George is interested, but when he hears the price, he says he's trying to save money, and that he might go along only for a drink.

Lennie and Carlson come back into the bunk house. Carlson puts his gun away, the dog dead. Curley quickly pops in, looking for his wife once again. He's suspicious of Slim, thinks that his wife was eyeing Slim, and wants to see if she's with him. Carlson and Whit think there's gonna be a fight and go outside to see if anything happens. George grills Lennie on what he saw outside. He wants to know what Slim was doing. Lennie tells George that Curley's wife wasn't anywhere near Slim, so it seems to George that there won't be any trouble.

Lennie begins to urge George to talk about the land they're gonna get one day again. George reminds him that they just talked about it last night, but Lennie wants to hear it again. As George talks, Candy listens in and wants to know how much the land will cost. George is initially distrustful, but tells the old man it'll be about $600. Candy confides that he'll have about $350 saved soon, and that they can go in on the land together. This is unexpected to George – he only has about $10 now and didn't expect to be able to get the land anytime soon. But now if he and Lennie worked for a while, they could get enough to buy the land pretty quick. The dreams which had always seemed far away in the future suddenly seem within reach.

Whenever George and Lennie discuss their dream, we really get to see the dream of the poor laborer – to be free, to be independent, to have no boss over you. To many it must seem like a nearly impossible dream, and to suddenly realize how close it is... it's almost overwhelming to George and Lennie. George begins to make plans, and orders the others to not say a word about their scheme to anyone.

The others return to the bunk house with Curley. Slim is angry at Curley for constantly pestering him about his wife, and Curley can't really get mad back because Slim hasn't done anything wrong. Angry, Curley sees Lennie smiling (still thinking about the dream farm and tending rabbits), and Curley lashes out at Lennie. Lennie tries to escape but has nowhere to go. Curley punches Lennie until George tells Lennie to fight back. Lennie grabs Curley's fist and crushes it. This ends the fight. They're gonna take Curley to a doctor, but first they get him to agree to say nothing. He's says that he'll tell his father and everyone else that his hand was crushed by a machine, not Lennie. And if he tries to get Lennie fired, they're all gonna band together against Curley and say what really happened, making him a laughing stock. Curley agrees to these terms and is taken to a doctor.

Lennie is concerned George will be mad at him, but he isn't. He did just what George told him to do. George tells him to go wash his face off – he's taken a good pounding.

**SECTION 4:** This section takes place in Crooks room next to the barn. As you may remember, Crooks is a black man with a crooked spine who's demonstrated a good deal of intelligence. His room is small, and connected to the barn. We get a detailed description of it. We also see that he has a gun. Crooks is described as generally aloof from the white men, but as we shall see, he is really quite lonely and longs for company.

It's Saturday night now, and the men, including George, have gone to the whorehouse in town. But Lennie has been left behind, and so has Candy. Lennie's been in the barn petting the puppies, and approaches Crooks room seeing the light, and Lennie begins to talk with Crooks. Crooks is initially defensive and doesn't want anyone in his room. But realizing Lennie's harmlessness, he lets the giant man come in. They begin talking and Lennie goes on and on about the land he's gonna get with George and Candy, forgetting in his excitement his promise to be silent. Crooks is cynical, believing that anything George says to Lennie really goes in one ear and out the other. To taunt Lennie a little,

Crooks speculates on what would become of Lennie if George should never return. The very concept of George abandoning him infuriates Lennie. Realizing his mistake, Crooks reassures him that he was only talking about himself. But Lennie has trouble seeing other people's point of view... he has a psychological immaturity that prevents it.

Crooks continues to talk about his loneliness and how it is to be an outsider on the ranch, the only black person around.

In talking about the land that Lennie goes on about, Crooks is also critical. He sees the dream as just that – a dream held by so many ranch workers, a dream never to be arrived at, like a faraway heaven.

At this point Candy comes in looking for Lennie. At first when he hears a sound Crooks thinks it's Slim, who he describes as "a real skinner" (a skinner is a mule driver). We can see how everyone on the farm has a respect for Slim.

Candy joins the two men in conversation in Crooks' room, initially uncomfortable. Crooks hears from Candy their plan for the dream ranch and Crooks laughs at them both as foolish. Candy doesn't like being laughed at and defends the plan, saying he already has the money. We can see that both Lennie and Candy are loose-lipped and lack George's cool head. George is the thinker of the group, but without him present both Lennie and Candy forget their promise. Since they seem to be serious about getting their own place after all, Crooks asks if he might be able to join them. I think this is the first time he's felt accepted in a long time, and he wants to get away from the life he's known.

They are interrupted as Curley's wife enters. She's looking for Curley, but not really. She knows he went to the whorehouse with the others. We can see that she is also lonely, and angry at Curley for being a dull, uncaring husband. She wants to know what really happened to Curley's hand. She doesn't believe the story about the machine accident and suspects Curley was really in a fight. She taunts the three men, provokes them, and even gets Candy to bring up the dream land again. Candy talks about it as thought they already have it, which they certainly do not. She taunts Candy some more, but Candy finally calms down and shuts up.

Curley's wife turns her attention to Lennie and notices the bruises on his face. When she asks what caused them, Lennie says, "He got his han' caught in a machine," essentially admitting through his clumsiness his involvement with Curley's damaged hand.

Crooks doesn't like the woman and her cunning ways and tries to get her out of his room, but she turns on him and takes advantage of her position as a white woman and threatens him. She could get him hanged, she says. And she could, with a simple accusation of a rude remark or an attempted rape – it would be a white woman's word against a black man, and her word would win out. Accepting her power over him, Crooks backs down.

They hear the sound of the men returning from town, and Curley's wife quickly leaves.

George enters the barn to find Lennie in Crooks' room and chastises Lennie for being there. When it becomes clear that Crooks has heard their plan to acquire their dream land, George chastises both Lennie and Candy for not being able to keep a secret. We see something interesting here with Crooks. Just a few minutes earlier he almost felt accepted and part of the group with Lennie and Candy. But with the barking anger of Curley's wife and now George, Crooks feels like the outsider once again, marginalized by white people. Crooks tells Candy that he was only joking about wanting to join them on their dream ranch.

The chapter ends with the white men returning to the bunk house.

**SECTION 5:** It's Sunday afternoon (remember that Lennie and George arrived on Friday). We begin the chapter inside the barn. The men have the day off for Sunday and are outside playing horseshoes. Lennie's the only one in the barn because he wants to be with the puppies, but as we zoom in on the scene we see that Lennie has accidentally killed a puppy that was too weak for his strong hands. He considers lying to George about the puppy, but he knows George is smart and will figure out what really happened. Now that the puppy is gone, he's angry at it for getting him into this dilemma. He feels certain now that George won't let him tend the rabbits on their dream ranch.

Curley's wife, always lurking about, enters the barn to talk with Lennie, and he's on guard. He remembers what George has told him —she is trouble. She persists in talking and sort of convinces him not to worry, because the men are far away playing horseshoes.

She talks about her life in Salinas growing up, about men who promised to make her famous, to put her in a show or take her to Hollywood and get her in the movies. One man promised to write her once her got to Hollywood, but she never heard from him. She's convinced that her mother stole the letter to keep her from going away. It seems a little more probable that the man simply didn't write, and only told her that to get what he wanted from her.

She had been angry about the situation, and went to a

dance at the Riverside Dance Palace and met Curley that night, and they soon married. We can see that she was restless and desperate to get away from the drab existence she'd known, and that marrying Curley was just a wild attempt to get away. She had a dream just like George and Lennie and Candy, but now she finds herself in a situation with Curley that is no improvement on her earlier life. All of these characters really want an escape from the life that faces them, and all are convinced that there's something more in life in the world than what they currently have.

Lennie doesn't know how to respond to her talk. Both Curley's wife and Lennie are largely self-absorbed and cannot really get out of their own heads. She gets angry when he talks about rabbits again, but asks him why he likes rabbits so much. It's because he likes soft things, and she agrees that soft things like silk are nice – so they do manage to find some common ground. She lets Lennie feel her hair because it is soft, and he really likes it. He gets too rough and she tries to make him stop, but he won't. This is an example of Lennie knowing something is wrong but being unable to resist his urges. She tries to get away from him, but he grabs her and tries to shut her up. Lennie doesn't want her screaming and getting him in trouble. He tells her not to yell and shakes her, and with his incredible strength he accidentally breaks her neck.

Lennie soon realizes what's he's done, that she is dead, and decides to leave and go to the hiding place agreed upon by him and George. He takes the dead puppy with him and leaves Curley's wife lying on the ground, half-covered by the hay.

The mother dog of of puppies (the "bitch") comes in soon after, and detects the dead woman and goes to her pups. Time seems to stop. It's an interim moment before the other characters realize what has occurred and Steinbeck sustains it in a beautiful way, letting it hover before the action begins again.

Finally, Candy enters the barn looking for Lennie. He finds Curley's wife there on the ground and thinks she is asleep, but then realizes that she is in fact dead. He goes and gets George and they quickly guess what has happened – that Lennie is responsible for killing her. Should they give Lennie time to get away? They discuss what to do, and one of Candy's first fears is that now they won't be getting their dream land after all. This is a pretty selfish thing to be thinking about when one character has been killed and another is in great danger. George starts to wonder if it was destined to be a dream, as if he always knew in his heart it would never come to pass.

George and Candy decide to tell the others. They need to catch Lennie. They agree to let George go back to the bunk house and act like he is hearing the news of the woman's death with all the others. Since he is connected with Lennie he wants to make sure it looks like he didn't know about the murder, and wasn't involved. So George leaves the barn.

Candy is alone with Curley's wife a minute, and he is angry at her. He blames her for what has happened, for stealing his dream away. Then he goes to tell the other men of her death.

They all return. The men gather around, and Slim confirms that she is dead by her broken neck.

Curley doesn't seem particularly saddened by this, but is completely enraged, and immediately suspects Lennie, since he was the only one not playing horseshoes. He wants to kill Lennie and goes to get his shotgun.

George also encourages Slim to lock up Lennie, but not to kill him. He has mental problems. But this is a time before a person's mental condition was really taken into account for a crime, particularly murder. When someone is killed, emotion rules the day, and it usually means "an eye for an eye."

Curley comes back with his gun. Carlson went to get his gun too, but it has disappeared. Carlson thinks Lennie took it because he just saw the gun that morning. They take Crooks gun to use as well.

Curley sends Whit to Soledad to get the police. He asks for Al Wilts, the deputy sheriff.

The men prepare to go hunt for Lennie, and Curley insists that George go along with them, so they don't think he had anything to do with it.

George encourages Curley not to kill Lennie, but Curley won't even consider it. He wants Lennie dead.

The tension is incredible at this point in the book. It has been building since we first met Curley. This is the book's rising action, leading to the climax. The suspense about what will occur is overwhelming. We have one chapter left, and it's inevitable that something dramatic will take place.

**SECTION 6:** It's late afternoon now, and this scene takes place where the first scene took place, along the river. Before any of the characters arrive we get this nature scene of a water snake being eaten by a bird. This can be seen as a reminder of life's brevity and cruelty.

Lennie arrives on the scene. He's clearly been rushing and is thirsty, so he takes a drink from the river. He starts to talk to himself. He's worried – but not so much about the law or Curley... no, what he's worried about is George's reaction to what he's done.

We begin to go into Lennie's mind and imagination.

His dead Aunt Clara appears before him and she tells Lennie to obey George in all things, and Lennie feels tremendous guilt because he realizes he has failed both George and his aunt.

Then a gigantic rabbit appears, and we understand that this is still all taking place in Lennie's mind – and it gives us an interesting look at how his mind works. The rabbit talks to Lennie and tells him why he'll never tend rabbits, and how George is going to punish him. But Lennie doesn't believe it and resists the giant rabbit angrily.

Then George appears... and after Aunt Clara and the giant rabbit (who are only in Lennie's mind) we may briefly wonder if this is *really* George, or just Lennie imagining George in his mind. But then other men are heard in the distance, and it becomes clear this really is George. He knew where Lennie would be hiding and found him before the others.

Lennie expects to be lectured and yelled at by his friend, but George is strangely resigned.

Lennie wants to hear George talk about the things he always talks about – he wants to hear George's sayings. George does so to appease Lennie, speaking calmly, resigned to what he must do. He asks Lennie to take his hat off, to enjoy the breeze, and tells Lennie once again about their dream land that they'll own. As he talks, George takes out a gun – Carlson's gun... we realize that George, not Lennie, was the one who took it.

Lennie doesn't see the gun, and George stands behind him. George tells Lennie to look across the river as he describes the dream ranch, the rabbits and so on. He aims the gun at the back of Lennie's head, and if we weren't clear what he had in mind, it's clear now. He means to kill Lennie himself. But he can't do it at first.

As George continues to talk and point his gun at the back of Lennie's head, the sound of the other men approaching is heard. Lennie is becoming overjoyed by George's talk, and at the height of his glee, George shoots him, killing him instantly. The quick death recalls the old dog killed earlier in the book: quick, but necessary.

Earlier in the book Old Candy couldn't kill his dog himself and let Carlson do it. In recognizing the necessity of Lennie's death, George has taken on the *responsibility* that Candy couldn't with the dog.

The other men soon arrive. Curley is satisfied now that Lennie is dead. Carlson still believes that Lennie took his gun, and that George somehow got it away from him to kill Lennie.

Slim is the only one who seems aware of the trauma involved for George to kill his friend, and offers to go with George to get a drink. Dazed, George agrees to go along and they head up toward the highway. As the others watch Slim and George go, Carlson says, "Now what the hell ya suppose is eatin' them two guys?"

And the book abruptly ends. We can see this last statement as an inability of many characters to see Lennie as a human being, with a childlike mind. Yes, he could get out of control, but George knows that as an adult he has a responsibility to Lennie, and we can speculate that he probably feels he failed in letting Lennie kill Curley's wife. In may have been necessary to kill Lennie, but not something George ever wanted.

# CONCLUSION

*Of Mice and Men* is a modern classic, as popular today as when it was first released. It unsettles us and asks difficult questions about how we live. I hope this guide has helped you navigate this book, and deepened your understanding of all that occurs in its pages.

Made in the USA
Middletown, DE
30 August 2018